PRINCESS WIGGLEBOTTOM
and the Forgotten Christmas

written by
Tia Martina

illustrated by
Patrick Laurent

Princess Wigglebottom and the Forgotten Christmas

Text copyright © 2021 Martina E. Faulkner
Illustrations copyright © 2021 Patrick Laurent

All rights reserved. No part of this publication may be reproduced or transmitted in any form or by any means, electronic or mechanical, including photocopying, recording, or any information storage and retrieval system, without express permission in writing from the publisher.

Distributed globally with Expanded Distribution by KDP.

ISBN Paperback: 978-1-953445-18-6
ISBN E-Book: 978-1-953445-19-3
Library of Congress Control Number: 2021948170

Inspirebytes Omni Media LLC
PO Box 988
Wilmette, IL 60091

For more information, please visit www.inspirebytes.com.

For Healey—the original "Princess Wigglebottom"—
who inspired me so many years ago and left us too early,
and for all the 'Wigglebottoms' in my life since,
especially Lucas and Maddie, who bring me joy every day
and remind me of what's truly important.

— Martina

To my family, Maya, Zane, Jude, and Veda:

Thanks so much for all your love and support.
Dreams do come true, so don't lose them.
Be brave and step into them.

— Patrick

It was early Christmas morning
A little before five,
Everyone was asleep,
And Santa Claus had arrived.

Princess Wigglebottom crept
Down the stairs on her own,
'Surely Santa left me a toy,
Or a bed, or a bone.'

She turned around the corner—
And much to her surprise—
She stared at the tree
And couldn't believe
her eyes!

'All these presents, these gifts
These stockings are so fine.
Surely something in there is for me,
Surely something is mine.'

She approached with caution,

As she began sniffing each box.

She opened something soft,
But it turned out to be socks!

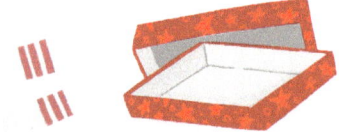

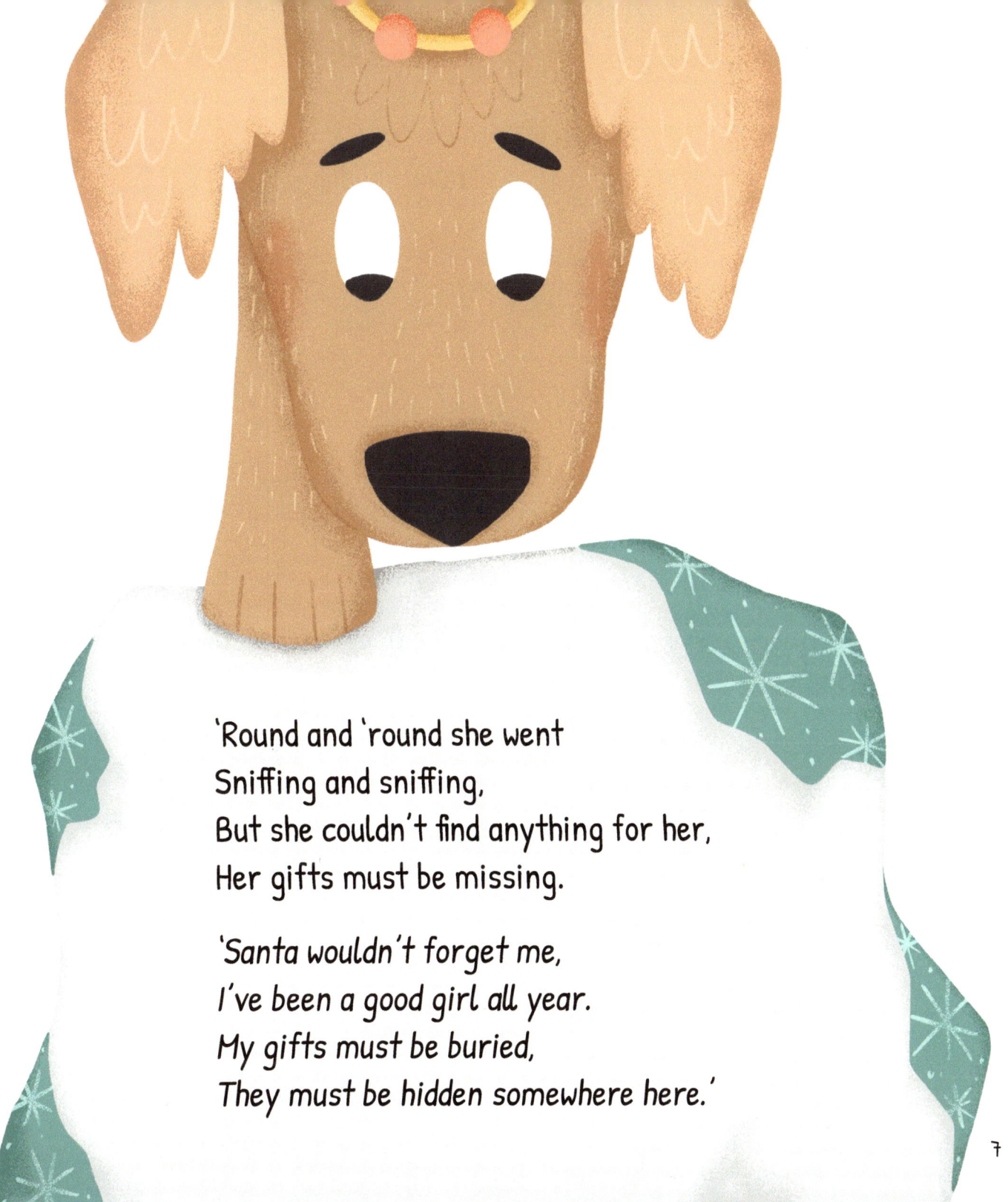

'Round and 'round she went
Sniffing and sniffing,
But she couldn't find anything for her,
Her gifts must be missing.

'Santa wouldn't forget me,
I've been a good girl all year.
My gifts must be buried,
They must be hidden somewhere here.'

So she dug a little deeper,
Opening a few gifts along the way.

She found Charlotte's new diary

And Michael's model made of clay.

She found Mamma's new
red sweater,
And Papa's new striped tie,
But with each gift she opened,
She wanted to cry.

'There's nothing for me.
I don't understand.
I've been a good girl.
I've learned to sit, stay, and stand.'

'I drink all my water,
and I eat all my food.
I get into a little mischief,
But basically, I'm good.'

'Why have I been forgotten?
Did I do something bad?'
Then she laid down in the presents,
Princess Wigglebottom was sad.

She fell asleep for a little while
Hidden under the tree.
Surrounded by the open presents,
She was such a sight to see!

Suddenly she woke up,
As she heard Mamma yell,

"PRINCESS WIGGLEBOTTOM!
You naughty, naughty girl!"

It was Mamma in her robe
Standing in front of the tree.
'But I thought,' thought Princess Wigglebottom,
'I thought something might be for me.'

"What were you thinking?"
"Why did you do it?"
"These presents were not yours."
"Now our Christmas is ruined!"

"BUT MAMMA,"

A little voice said from behind.
It was Michael in his pajamas
At the age of just nine.

"Maybe Princess Wigglebottom
Was just helping out —
Or I think, could it be,
She was feeling a bit left out?"

"Did Santa leave her a gift?
After all, she's been quite good.
She's our family, our best friend..."
And with that Princess Wigglebottom stood.

She walked over to Michael
Past the tie and the sweater.
It seemed, after all,
That Santa did not forget her.

She had a family who loved her,
Who was kind and forgiving.
She felt grateful for everything
That she had been given.

She felt sorry that she had ruined
Their Christmas morning that day,
And she showed her regret
By tucking her tail away.

Michael knelt down and hugged her
And told her not to be upset,
For Christmas was about family
And that included the "pet."

With that she was happy
And her tail started to wag,
Which wiggled her bottom
And made Michael laugh.

As she watched them, Mamma said,
'Michael, you're quite right.'
But Michael had stopped laughing,
Because he spotted something white.

With a big red ribbon
That was tied in a bow,
It was hidden behind the tree,
Underneath the window.

He reached for the present and pulled it straight out,
Then turned to Princess Wigglebottom with a smile and a shout:

"Look Princess Wigglebottom! What do you see?
It's not a present for Mamma, and it's not a present for me."

Michael held up the gift,
As Mamma smiled and giggled.
Then Princess Wigglebottom barked,
"Woof, Woof!" and she wiggled.

'A bone! A bone!' she thought,
As she barked with delight.
'I haven't been forgotten —
It was just tucked out of sight!'

Then Princess Wigglebottom settled down
With her bone in a bow,
As the rest of the family woke up
And the excitement began to grow.

"Merry Christmas!"
"Good Morning!"
"What a wonderful day!"
"I love you." and "Thank you."
Were the words they would say.

After everything was opened
And they said thank you for their gifts,
They hugged Princess Wigglebottom
Who smiled and sniffed.

Because there's nothing like Christmas
To remind us with love,
That there's nothing like family
And that includes everyone.

ABOUT THE AUTHOR
Tia Martina

Tia Martina is author Martina Faulkner's alter-ego, a name born of her love for her countless nieces and nephews, both biological and relational. For over two decades, "Tia Martina" has been synonymous with fun, hugs, and love — as well as a good story or two.

When Martina is not writing, she can be found helping other writers and artists in developing their own work. Originally from New York, Martina lives outside Chicago where she loves spending time in nature with her dogs.

Learn more about Martina at tiamartina.com.

ABOUT THE ILLUSTRATOR
Patrick Laurent

Patrick Laurent is the creative artist behind *Laurent Collective*. He began his career in art when he was in elementary school, drawing and creating sports characters and selling them to his friends. He has gone on to create a body of work that can be found in homes across the globe through art prints, apparel, homeware, and books.

Patrick is from Indiana and now lives and works in London with his family. His aim is to create work that reminds everyone that they have something unique to offer the world.

Learn more about Patrick at laurentcollective.com.

www.ingramcontent.com/pod-product-compliance
Lightning Source LLC
Chambersburg PA
CBHW041059070526
44579CB00002B/15